Original title:
The Tangle of Tassels

Copyright © 2025 Creative Arts Management OÜ
All rights reserved.

Author: Harris Montgomery
ISBN HARDBACK: 978-1-80586-205-5
ISBN PAPERBACK: 978-1-80586-677-0

Heavy with History

In a cupboard sits a scarf,
Full of stories, full of laughs.
Each fray a tale, each knot a joke,
Persistent threads, like an old bloke.

A history wrapped in colorful threads,
Dancing around like silly heads.
Whispers of yesteryears float about,
In the fabric, giggles we shout.

Silken Shadows

Silk ties lurking in the night,
Growing in number, a silly sight.
They dance around, play hide and seek,
Whispering secrets; oh, how they speak!

Twists and turns through the hallway glide,
Turning the mundane into a ride.
With every turn, a laugh we share,
As shadows play games with colors rare.

Braids of Bravery

Braiding hair like a twisty vine,
Each loop a venture, oh, how divine!
With laughter echoing down the hall,
Each strand tells tales of bravery's call.

A beehive, a braid, or a wild twist,
Creativity blooms, there's no way to resist.
It's serious fun, just don't pull too tight,
Or you might find yourself in a hair-raising plight!

Lost in the Weave

In the loom, where chaos resides,
Threads get tangled, oh how they slide.
A patchwork world of colors and dreams,
Where nothing unraveled is quite what it seems.

A warp and a weft, a nod and a wink,
This frayed masterpiece makes you think:
When lost in the magic, just laugh it away,
For weaving the wild is where we play!

Embraces of Texture

Fuzzy friends dance in the breeze,
Laughter echoes, tangled with ease.
Colors collide, a mismatched play,
Threads of humor lead us astray.

Lumpy knots in a fabric fight,
Frolicking fibers, oh what a sight!
Silly stitches can't hide the fun,
Knots of joy, we laugh as we run.

Intertwined Wishes

Wishful threads in a yarny mess,
Dreams knotted tight, it's anyone's guess.
Patterns mixed in a playful cheer,
Each loop and twist draws us near.

Hopes wrapped up in vibrant spools,
Wondrous whims of color in pools.
Tickled pink by the threads we choose,
Fancies frolic, we just can't lose.

Flaws in Fabric

Patchwork chaos, oh what a sight,
Quirky patches fit just right.
Stitches wobbly, yet full of glee,
Flaws make this cloth uniquely free.

Sloppy seams, but who really cares?
Laughter woven through all our hares.
Misfit moments, a tapestry bright,
In each odd flaw, we find delight.

Crossed Lines of Love

Lines are crossed in a playful game,
Wobbly paths, yet nothing's the same.
Knotty connections between our hearts,
Humorous twirls, where laughter starts.

String by string, our stories unfold,
With each rough twist, a treasure to hold.
Tangled tales of affection and cheer,
In this wild weave, we dance without fear.

Threads of Serenity

In a basket of yarn, colors entwined,
Kittens all frolic, their mischief aligned.
One sneaks a ball, it rolls under chairs,
While the other one pounces, no worry, no cares.

Knots found in laughter, a giggle or two,
As needles take flight, like a stitch in a shoe.
One thread goes this way, the other goes that,
Creating a scarf, or maybe a hat.

Fabrics of Identity

A patchwork of dreams, sewn with delight,
Torn jeans and old shirts, a splendid sight.
Mom said it's fashion, I smiled and I spun,
In a rainbow of mishaps, I'm the quirky one.

Ties that we wear, with patterns askew,
Stripes clash with dots, a bold look, it's true.
Each thread tells a tale, with laughs we adore,
In this crazy wardrobe, there's always room for more.

Ties of Turmoil

Shoelaces tangled, a two-sport affair,
One's stuck to a chair, the other in hair.
Spinning around, like a top on the run,
Who knew getting dressed could be this much fun?

Belt loops in chaos, slipping and sliding,
Trying to fit in, while giggling and hiding.
But oh! when we trip, laughter's the norm,
In this whirlwind of fabric, we dance in the storm.

Loopy Laments

Around and around, the thread keeps on crying,
Loopy and tangled, but oh, how it's trying!
Stitch by stitch, we patch up the pain,
With a twist of humor, it's never in vain.

Crochet hooks poke with a curtsy of sass,
Loops on the left side extend to the past.
A misfit creation, a hat for a cat,
With frills and with fluffs, who could argue with that?

Bound by Twists

In a world of strings and loops,
A cat finds joy in tangled troops.
With every pull, a giggle burst,
As yarn becomes a playful curse.

Two friends laugh at every mess,
Knots and twists bring more distress.
Yet in this chaos, joy is spun,
Life's little tangles can be fun!

Symphony of Knots

A ukulele lost in fray,
Strings crossed, they dance and sway.
Each pluck a note of wild delight,
In this chaos, music takes flight.

A ball of yarn rolls down the lane,
Chasing laughter, crazy and vain.
With every tug, a new refrain,
Knots are here, but joy remains!

Echoes of the Woven Path

On a journey through strands and ties,
A sock goes missing, oh, what a surprise!
Wandering shoes with no clear plan,
Feet are left in quite a jam.

The twists and turns start to spin,
A game of hide and seek begins.
With every twist, a chuckle grows,
In this maze, where fun just flows.

Fabric of Forgotten Whispers

A quilt adorned with tales untold,
Hiding secrets, both warm and bold.
Every patch is a laugh or tear,
Stitched with memories that we share.

Fabrics tangled, colors collide,
Each thread a story, side by side.
In this jumble, smiles appear,
Woven wonders that we hold dear.

The Silhouette of Strings

In a corner sat a spool,
With threads that danced, and threads that drool.
They twisted left, then right, a mess,
A fiber fool in total stress.

One day a cat came to play,
Chasing shadows, bright and gay.
She leapt and pounced, a crafty thief,
Threading chaos, much to my grief.

Now there's a fabric of delight,
In colors wild, a true sight.
From tangled webs, we both did weave,
A quilt of laughs, we won't believe.

Loops of Longing

Beneath the couch, a fluffy ball,
Of yarn so bright, it caught my call.
It needled dreams of knit and purl,
Yet tangled toes, made me want to hurl.

Alas, each loop took on a life,
It danced with glee, avoiding strife.
My cat, perplexed, gave a fitting glance,
As rainbow yarn began to prance.

In every twist, a story spun,
Of rogue threads escaping just for fun.
Embrace the mess, it's all in jest,
A tapestry of laughter, at best.

Patterns in Disarray

Oh, the weaver with a frown,
Found his threads all turned around.
Stitches looped in an odd embrace,
A pattern lost, a race to chase.

His schema fled, his plan went awry,
A patchwork quilt soared up to the sky.
Each frayed end sang a silly tune,
As colors clashed like a loony moon.

Yet in this jumble, pure delight,
Jestful chaos painted night.
No right or wrong in this mad play,
Just echoes of laughter woven each day.

Tales of Twisted Yarn

Gather 'round for a yarn so bold,
Of fibers tangled, stories told.
Each skein has its own wild tale,
Of knotted dreams that set to sail.

A sock that lost its partner gone,
And ribbons that danced from dusk till dawn.
Each loop embraced a giggling fate,
Leaving laughter in its wake, first-rate.

In knots they find their merry way,
A quirky fate, come what may.
So cast aside neatness, don't scorn,
In the playful mess, we all are reborn.

Fleeting Fibers

Threads of laughter fly around,
A rainbow dance, no strings are bound.
Each spin a joke, a twist, a tease,
Like socks that vanish with such ease.

A fabric adventure on the go,
Knots are hiding, oh what a show!
A stitch of chaos, bright and free,
Who knew yarn could be so silly?

The Knotting of Hearts

Two hearts entwined with frayed designs,
Hilarious missteps, tangled lines.
A quirky bind, a knit so rare,
Love's crafted chaos fills the air.

Laughter echoes through the thread,
With every loop, more joy is bred.
A playful weave, a jolly spree,
In every knot, a mystery!

Boundless Textures

Textures jumbled, oh what a mix,
Like mismatched socks in playful tricks.
A prickly patch with silky swirls,
Where every fiber dances, twirls.

The woolly whimsy takes a leap,
Wrapped in patterns, secrets keep.
Each pattern a giggle, a soft surprise,
Boundless laughter as it flies!

Weave of Wanderlust

A tapestry bright with questing dreams,
Each color a chuckle, bursting seams.
Adventurers stitch with glee and flair,
Where patterns hop, and wanderers dare.

From yarn-balls rolling, goofy and round,
To scarves that love the lost and found.
A playful weave of silly fights,
In every stitch, a world ignites!

Threads of Tomorrow

In a world where yarns unite,
A cat steals wool with pure delight.
Knots and loops in playful cheer,
Who knew they'd end up tangled here?

One sweater shrinks, who could foresee?
My grandma's scarf, now fit for a bee.
Threads of future tangled tight,
We laugh at all the silly sight!

Crossing Cords

Two cords meet in a jolly dance,
They trip and stumble, what a chance!
Knotting fools amidst the glee,
Who knew making messes could set us free?

A sock goes missing, oh what a tale,
Left behind, it begins to wail.
A tug-of-war with every thread,
Turns into laughs, forgetting dread!

Tresses and Tales

Long strands of hair, they twist and twine,
Each telling stories, oh so divine.
A braid gone rogue, it takes a spin,
Laughing as it pulls my chin.

Combing through tales of hair-brush plight,
Swapping woes in the soft moonlight.
From messy buns to curls set free,
In laughter we find this hair-istry!

Bonds in Every Stitch

With needles clicking, we dive right in,
Creating bonds through every spin.
Oh dear, a sweater's now a vest,
But in our hearts, it's still the best!

A patchwork quilt of friendship sewn,
Each little stitch, a love well-known.
Through laughter's weave we will entwine,
Forever cozy, your hand in mine!

The Chaos Within the Weave

In a closet hung a sock,
A pair that surely could not mock.
One went left, the other right,
Yet both are lost, oh what a sight!

The curtain's frayed, the couch a mess,
Chasing threads brings little stress.
Laughter rings as they unwound,
A jumble of color all around.

A loopy yarn joined in the fun,
Made a scarf for everyone.
It twirled and danced, a playful swirl,
Each stitch a giggle, each knot a twirl.

In every weave, a tale to spin,
Of crafty chaos, let's begin.
Though knots may tease and brushes clash,
We giggle through the fabric's trash.

Cords of Connection

Two strings meet at random's call,
One plays the flute, the other a brawl.
Together they dance in knotty glee,
Oh what a pair, just let them be!

In tangled lines, friendships brew,
They laugh and snicker, a lively crew.
One says "tight," the other says "loose,"
That's how connections are made profuse.

When cord meets cord, sparks ignite,
A chronicle born of sheer delight.
Missteps abound, but no one's mad,
For cords of connection aren't all that bad.

They weave a tale of silly slips,
With playful crisscrossed, daring flips.
In every twist, a joyous song,
Together they flourish, where they belong.

Fragile Moments Entangled

A spider's web, oh what a prank,
Glistening soft on the garden plank.
It catches laughter, it holds a sigh,
Fragile moments floating by.

In the wind they spin, these threads so meek,
Each a story, some quirky, some cheek.
They tangle up in a giddy blur,
Like kids on swings, oh what a stir!

When life gets knotted, just take a break,
Have a giggle, for fun's own sake.
With every twist, a smile will show,
Entangled moments, don't say no!

So dance with the threads of possibility,
To find humor in the fragility.
For tangled laughter is truly grand,
A shared moment, hand in hand.

Threads of Fate

In the loom of life, we weave our fate,
With quirky turns, we navigate.
A blue thread laughs, a red one glows,
Mix them up, and who really knows?

Each pattern forms with every twist,
Yet who can tell what we've missed?
With jokes in stitches, we trim the fray,
As fate pulls us in, we dance and play.

So grab a strand, let's make it bright,
We'll knot our dreams in pure delight.
Hop on the fabric of silly fate,
And laugh at threads that cannot wait!

For in this weave, joy intertwines,
In every color, each twist defines.
Life's a canvas, let's paint it gay,
With threads of fate, we'll find our way.

Silken Entanglements

A ball of yarn rolled away,
Chasing it seemed like a play.
Cats and dogs join the chase,
In this glorious, tangled space.

Laughter echoes, hearts are light,
Knots are formed from sheer delight.
Each twist and turn brings a grin,
As we trip and tumble in spin.

A ribbon tied around my shoe,
A dance disaster, who knew?
Slips and slides on colors bright,
Such a joyful, silly sight.

Like a jigsaw puzzle askew,
Every tangle, just a clue.
In this maze of fuzzy threads,
We find humor, life, and spreads.

Weaving Through the Past

Memories wrapped in mismatched thread,
Came unspooled as I laughed and bled.
Grandma's scarf with a funky design,
Had stories woven, each one a sign.

Tangled tales of days gone by,
With a wink and a silly sigh.
Socks left alone, never confined,
Seeking their mates, all intertwined.

Old photos pinned with safety pins,
Remind me of my foolish wins.
Dancing with shadows, giggling loud,
In this tangled mess, we're all proud.

Past and present, a comic mix,
Each knot a tale, life's great tricks.
We navigate with giggles vast,
Through the fabric of our past.

Colors of Confusion

Crimson, teal, and shades of green,
A canvas splashed, what a scene!
Just one brush, a wild spree,
Creates a riot of laughter, you see.

Socks of yellow with purple ties,
Look like disco balls when they fly.
Mismatched shoes on a joyful jog,
Every step like a dancing fog.

Stripes with polka dots unite,
A fashion faux pas shines so bright!
Confused but cheerful, we embrace,
Each color clash fills the space.

In this spectrum that we wear,
Funny faces everywhere.
Life's a circus, loud and bold,
Colors of confusion never old.

Frayed and Twisted

Strings from my hoodie, loose and free,
Create a masterpiece of folly.
Each fray tells a story untold,
Of mishaps and laughter, pure gold.

Sneaking snacks while wearing a scarf,
Ends up resembling a graph.
The more I eat, the tighter it grips,
Accidental hugs, life's friendly quips.

Twisted tales of tangled fate,
Every wobble, we celebrate.
Like a dance with shoes gone askew,
Every misstep, something new.

In the chaos, we find our fun,
A game of threads never done.
Frayed and twisted, yes indeed,
Life's a laugh, it's all we need.

Threads of Time

In a cupboard, chaos reigns,
Stray threads dance in silly lanes.
A sock's misplaced, where could it be?
I swear it grew legs and fled from me!

Buttons roll like tiny cars,
Stitching dreams beneath the stars.
A needle pokes at threads of fate,
Crafting laughter, it can't be late!

Interwoven Echoes

With patterns twisted, smiles ensue,
A yarn's adventure, oh so askew.
Loops and whirls in crazy spins,
A hat so big, where do I begin?

In stitches tight, the giggles burst,
As I untangle, I quench my thirst.
The fabric sings its clumsy tune,
Dancing threads beneath the moon.

The Knotting Hour

Knots tied tight in a silly game,
The more I pull, the more I blame.
Colors clash, a vibrant fright,
As I wrestle with fabric and light.

A yarn ball rolls across the floor,
Like a puppy, it begs for more.
Every twist, a chuckle near,
As I craft, I dance with cheer!

Fragments of Fabric

Tiny patches tell their tale,
Each with humor, each with rail.
A quilt of dreams so threadbare,
Looks like a puzzle without a care.

Threads in loops, a messy scene,
Like spaghetti, oh so keen!
With every pull, the laughter spreads,
In this fabric, whimsy threads!

Knots in Time

A ball of yarn rolled down the lane,
Chasing a cat through the pouring rain.
With every twist, a giggle escapes,
As they trip and tumble like clumsy drapes.

Grandma's knitting, a puzzling sight,
Her needles dance like stars at night.
A scarf that started as just a thread,
Now a masterpiece, or so she said!

The more she knits, the more it twists,
A pretzel shawl that couldn't exist.
She laughs and sighs at the tangled spree,
"Maybe I'll just let it be!"

With every knot a story congeals,
Of yarny mishaps and silly squeals.
Time marches on, with stitches anew,
And the laughter echoes through every hue.

Captured in Fiber

In a world where colors collide,
Yarn takes flight, a whimsical ride.
A squirrel in a sweater, oh what a sight,
Frolicking freely with pure delight.

Loop after loop, they craft some funk,
A sock puppet dance, with the aid of junk.
"Look at the cat in a knitted cap!"
A chorus of laughter, and it's all a trap!

Wooly warriors join the fun,
Battling with yarn, 'til the day is done.
Captured in fiber, each silly pose,
A masterpiece born from chaos that grows.

With every stitch a chuckle grows,
Knitting camaraderie, who knows how it goes?
The tangled threads, a merry band,
Creating nonsense, perfectly unplanned.

Patterns of Perseverance

With needles clicking, the clock chimes loud,
In a room full of yarn, she feels so proud.
Patterns dancing in her head so bright,
Yet somehow they twist, oh what a sight!

Patterns of perseverance morph to game,
A cheeky challenge, but who's to blame?
As stitches skip and yarns do fly,
A grandma giggles, "Oh my, oh my!"

A blanket that doubles as a circus tent,
The cat is trapped, with no intent.
She shakes her head, and with a grin,
Adds a few more rows and lets chaos in.

With every mistake comes laughter's cheer,
This knitted journey brings us near.
So here's to the patterns that twist and wind,
May humor and warmth be forever entwined!

Twists of Abandon

A skein of yarn rolls out the door,
With a giggle and a hop, it seeks adventure more.
It spirals and twirls over lawn and bush,
Leaving a sight that may cause a hush.

Knots forming wildly in the tall grass,
As birds look on, they think, "What a class!"
A creature wraps itself, looking quite proud,
In yarny glory, shouting out loud!

Twists of abandon make chaos bloom,
A dance of colors that brightens the gloom.
The neighbors peek out, scratching their heads,
Not knowing the fun that joyfully spreads.

Yet in this tangle, a message rings clear,
Life's not complete without a touch of cheer.
With every twist, may laughter unfurl,
In the delightful madness of this wooly whirl!

Cords of Continuity

Twisted wires dance and sway,
Entangled threads in a game to play.
A rabbit found, with shoes askew,
He leaps for joy, but trips right too!

In every knot, a giggling sound,
A playful yarn that wraps around.
The more you pull, the tighter it gets,
Like uncle Bob's wild fishing nets!

Threads of Solitude

A solitary thread, lost in space,
Trying to find its complex place.
It wriggles and squirms, a one-man show,
But oh, how tangled into trouble it'll grow!

A needle looks on, with a wink of glee,
As the thread swirls in a dance so free.
"Join my crew," the needle does jest,
"Or stay there alone, it's a tangled fest!

Stitching Silhouettes

In shadows cast by crafty hands,
Stitches groove in funny bands.
A funny face starts to appear,
With button eyes and a friendly cheer!

Each stitch a giggle, a laugh, a sigh,
As the silhouette wishes to fly high.
But tied to fabric, it can't escape,
One silly grin, what a funny shape!

Ropes of Remembrance

Ropes recalling fun-filled days,
All the laughter and quirky plays.
Each twist and turn, a story to tell,
Of picnic fails and a very loud yell!

Pulled tight between memories past,
A tug of war, hold on, hold fast!
With every knot, a giggle profound,
In the ropes of life, humor is found!

Knotted Dreams

In a drawer, ribbons hide,
Twisted tales of pride.
A cat pounced, oh what fun!
Now chaos has begun!

Colors clash, a playful sight,
Knots that giggle in moonlight.
A butterfly joins the fray,
Dancing in a yarn ballet.

Threads entwined, a tangled mess,
Yet laughter brings a sweet caress.
With every tug, a funny squeal,
These mishaps make the best appeal!

So let us laugh, and weave anew,
In knots of joy, just me and you.

Ribbons of Resilience

Ribbons twirling in the breeze,
Swaying, laughing through the trees.
One snagged high upon a limb,
Is it magic, or a whim?

Colors bright, a playful fight,
Tangled up, we find delight.
A cat rolls by, oh what a scene,
Spectacle of colors, bright and keen!

A father shouts, 'Come set me free!'
But the knots are stuck, oh dear me!
A trip, a fall, the laughter swells,
All thanks to our ribboned spells!

Through every twist, a grin appears,
We celebrate with silly cheers!

Weaving Whispers

In the attic, whispers spin,
Old tales that make us grin.
A ghostly ribbon, bold and bright,
Floats along, a silly flight.

Threads of laughter laced with glee,
Here, let's weave our mystery!
Every pull, a story's tease,
Even the spider chuckles, please.

An old sock, a funky hat,
Who knew yarn could talk like that?
With every twist, a giggle grows,
These antics only yarn can expose!

In this web, our joy is spun,
Weaving whispers, all in fun.

Twisted Journeys

A roll of yarn is quite a trip,
It begins with just a single whip!
But as we pull, oh what a craze,
Now it's a dance, in so many ways!

Chasing tails, oh don't you fall,
A tumble, twist, it laughs at all.
Hats fly high, and socks take flight,
These crafty journeys bring delight!

A kitten hops, with eyes so round,
Amongst the chaos, joy is found.
We thread the fun, with every spin,
In twisted tales, we laugh and grin!

So grab your yarn and squeeze it tight,
Let's travel on this thread tonight!

Fabrications of Fate

In a world where threads collide,
Laughter weaves on every side.
A knotty puzzle, tangled cheer,
Where fabric dreams draw us near.

Quilts decide our dance today,
Spinning tales in a quirky way.
Socks and ties in odd delight,
Crafting chaos day and night.

String of fate, a playful game,
Each twist provided a new name.
Frayed edges giggle with such glee,
Who knew yarn could set us free?

So grab a stitch and join the fun,
In patched-up tales, we become one.
Fabricated chuckles make us sway,
In this wild weave, we'll laugh all day.

Bound by Design

Patterns clash, a lively sight,
Three-legged races in the night.
Thread and thumb twirl with a grin,
As fabric follies start to spin.

Each strand that binds us makes us reel,
In stitches and seams, we feel surreal.
A bow misplaced, a clip askew,
Fashion faux pas, but who knew?

Tangled laces in stealthy shoes,
Chasing giggles, we can't refuse.
Outfits clash in colors bright,
Roving revelers, what a sight!

Design's a dance, a whimsical chase,
In this amusing, tangled space.
We strut our stuff, hats high in air,
Bound by laughter, without a care.

Unearthed Textiles

Hidden secrets in fabric old,
Stories wait to be retold.
Patterns rustle, whisper and tease,
Unearthed treasures bring us ease.

Ruffled edges, a fashion crime,
Twisted tales, oh, isn't it prime?
Old curtains sway, a dance of dreams,
As each fray bursts at the seams.

Faded quilts tell jokes of yore,
Threads unwind, we laugh for sure.
Jumbled notions, patchwork of fun,
Stories unraveled by everyone.

A fiber feast, we dine on glee,
In tangled textiles, wild and free.
Each stitch a giggle, each seam a grin,
In this quirky fabric, we all fit in!

Twisted Interpretations

What's that design? A riddle spun,
A shirt that thinks it's a ton of fun.
Round and round, the plaid goes mad,
In a fashion show, it's sure to be rad.

Hats that wobble, pom-poms askew,
Jackets that wink, just for you.
A scarf that dances in silly loops,
Giggling garments and lively troops.

Each layer woven with playful flair,
Hosting a carnival in the air.
Tangled laughter, a jumbled spree,
Interpreted wild, just wait and see.

Socks that mismatch, shirts that clash,
While fashion trends go by in a flash.
In this zany fabric, we all delight,
Twisted hilarity, oh what a sight!

The Hidden Fibers

In the corner, a sock with a hole,
Threads are dancing, on a roll.
A tangle of colors, bright and bold,
Stories of laundry mishaps told.

A red string winks at a blue,
Whispers secrets, just us two.
Beneath the basket, chaos reigns,
Who knew socks had such wild chains?

A fuzzy ball rolls down the hall,
Caught on a chair, oh dear, you fall!
Each twist and loop brings a laugh,
In this realm, we craft our path.

So here's to fibers, tangled tight,
Making mischief, oh what a sight!
In laughter we weave, a silly tale,
Of socks and threads on a grand scale.

A Tapestry of Secrets

Once I found a secret thread,
It looped and swirled, like it was fed.
It whispered tales of hidden dreams,
In the fabric of life, nothing's as it seems.

A patchwork quilt of quirky sights,
With every stitch, it ignites lights.
A button hitches a ride on a yarn,
Incognito, plotting its charm!

Patterns collide, colors vie,
A fabric party makes you sigh.
With a snicker here and a giggle there,
We unfurl fabrics, laughter in the air.

Who needs a map when threads conspire?
With every tangle, they'll take you higher.
In our weaving games, all secrets unfold,
In the tapestry of life, laughs are gold.

Cables of Memory

Tangled wires, oh what a mess,
Charging dreams in a funny dress.
Each twist a story, each knot a jest,
With every poke, I feel blessed.

A charger fights with a pair of keys,
Finding power brings silent pleas.
A memory card whispers, 'Hey, remember?'
It juggles moments like a humorous member.

In tangled cables, the past resides,
Funny faces in memory slides.
With each frustration, a chuckle springs,
In the chaos of life, joy still sings.

So when your gadgets decide to play,
Just sit back, laugh, and save the day.
For in every loop and every twist,
Lies a memory that can't be missed.

Winding Roads Beneath

Under the couch, what do I find?
A missing shoe, my cat unkind.
Winding roads of dust bunnies roam,
In my living room, chaos is home.

A paper clip takes a daring leap,
Over old snacks, secrets creep.
What adventures these pathways claim,
Roads of laughter, no two the same.

Tangled cords like spaghetti night,
Trying to find the end feels light.
Every twist is a winding chase,
In this maze, laughter finds its place.

So here we wander, paths in surprise,
Under the surface, much to analyze.
Life's a journey, humorous and wild,
In the winding roads, we're all a child.

Echoed Textures

In a room with threads a-clatter,
A sock tangled up with a platter.
Laughter spins in every hue,
As the cat joins in on the stew.

Chasing colors, what a sight,
Brighter than a disco night.
Mismatched patterns dance and wiggle,
In this fabric, chuckles giggle.

With each twist and loop we find,
Silly patterns tie the mind.
Who knew threads could spin such tales,
As laughter sails with fluffy sails?

Nine colors of socks and a shoe,
Who knew chaos could be so true?
With every knot and every seam,
Fabric giggles, weaving a dream.

A Fabric of Dreams

In a world where pajamas rule,
Every fabric makes us drool.
Cotton clouds and silk so bright,
Tickle fights by morning light.

Button eyes on a shirt parade,
Each patch tells a joke, well played.
Knotty friends from the back of drawers,
Now they're rolling on the floors.

Spools of laughter dressed in style,
Tracing smiles across the mile.
Woolly sheep sing silly songs,
In this fabric where joy belongs.

Glitter threads in every seam,
Together here, we can dream.
In tangled knots, we find our fun,
A fabric dance for everyone.

Entangled Joy

Strings of laughter fill the air,
As mismatched socks hang without care.
Blended patterns, oh, what a sight,
A fashion faux pas that feels so right!

Three shirts and a hat, what a mix,
Fashion faux pas that never sticks.
Chuckling caps with floppy ears,
Woven silliness of the years.

Dresses spin like whirling tops,
Among the buttons and rubber drops.
With every twist, the giggles rise,
An outfit made of laughs and sighs.

Ruffled edges, a cuddly mess,
Making peace with fabric stress.
In all this yarn, we find delight,
Entangled joy, ready to ignite.

Woven Whimsy

Threads of mischief intertwine,
In a fabric where giggles shine.
Colors twirl, a merry dance,
Each thread echoes a silly chance.

The quilt speaks of tales untold,
Warm embraces, and laughter bold.
Pillow fights and blanket races,
Where every stitch a smile embraces.

Crazy patterns tell a tale,
Of socks that plot and shirts that sail.
Dancing threads under the sun,
In woven madness, we have fun.

Knit together, a jolly spree,
Every fabric laughs with glee.
In this whimsy, we all belong,
Woven together, we sing our song.

A Dance of Fray

In a room where threads collide,
The socks have gathered, side by side.
With mismatched patterns, they do sway,
In this quirky, silly ballet.

The buttons roll with much delight,
While zippers zip with sheer delight.
A frayed old scarf joins in the fun,
As laughter dances, one by one.

A beaded bracelet starts to twirl,
And ribbons spin in whirls and curls.
Among this chaos, joy takes flight,
A party made of strings so bright.

So grab your yarn, don't be shy,
Let tangles fly and chaos lie.
For in this mess, the fun's not far,
Together we'll outshine a star.

Loose Ends of Life

In a world where fibers roam,
The stray threads never find a home.
A shoelace dangling from a shoe,
Wonders just what it should do.

Wires waltz in a jumbled line,
Tangled cords, oh what a sign!
With every twist and every bend,
A story waits at every end.

Paperclips in daisy chains,
Counting all the tiny gains.
With each loose end that we find,
A giggle forms within the mind.

So grab your strands and weave your tale,
Let chaos echo, never pale.
For life's a mess wrapped in a bow,
And giggles grow where tangles flow.

Tapestry of Stories

In the weaver's colorful booth,
Stitching tales of funny truth.
Yarns entangled, tales misread,
A purr of laughter where it's spread.

A patch of plaid meets polka dots,
The saga grows, oh what a plot!
With every loop, a chuckle bursts,
As they spin tales, or rather, worsts.

The needle's point is sharp and sly,
Creativity begins to fly.
A patchwork quilt that tells a joke,
With every poke, it starts to poke.

So take your thread and give a twirl,
Let knots form into laughter's whirl.
For in this fabric, rich and bright,
Stories weave in pure delight.

Unraveled Secrets

Beneath the chair, a mystery lies,
In tangled skeins, the laughter flies.
What secrets do those yarns conceal?
A puzzle spun that's hard to peel.

A ball of twine starts to unwind,
Revealing tidbits of the mind.
The cat leaps in, a furry thief,
Unraveling joy, beyond belief.

And there among the chaos sprawls,
A tale of life in patterned calls.
As threads unravel, visions blend,
Each knot, a memory to mend.

So let them roll, those messy threads,
With giggles bursting from our heads.
For in this jumbled, silly spree,
The secrets laugh, and so do we.

Whispers of Frayed Threads

In a cupboard where socks rarely meet,
Lives a thread who dreams of a dance so sweet.
It tangles and twirls with a quirky flair,
A fashion disaster, but it doesn't care.

Once it joined forces with a button so round,
Together they made a most humorous sound.
They rolled and they flipped, oh what a sight,
Two misfit pals, twinkling in delight.

One day a shoelace decided to see,
If it could join in, oh, wouldn't that be glee?
But in the chaos, it tripped and it fell,
They giggled so hard, ringing a bell.

So next time you find a thread out of line,
Remember the joy in a twist and a twine.
For every odd tangle spins tales of cheer,
In a world filled with laughter, there's nothing to fear.

Knots of Memory

Grandma's yarn sits, all knotted and bright,
Each twist a secret, each tangle a fight.
She swore it was magic, she wore out her hook,
Turning chaos to comfort with every nook.

The cat loves to play with the ends just for fun,
Chasing the threads like a race in the sun.
She pounces and tangles, oh what a scene,
It's a feline ballet, silly but keen.

Then there's Uncle Bob, with his big clumsy hands,
He picked up the chaos, all tied in strands.
"Look!" he exclaimed, "I made a new chair!"
Well, it wobbled and squeaked, but nobody cared.

Each thread tells a story, a giggle or sigh,
With knots that remind us of years passing by.
So gather your yarn, let the laughter unfold,
In a world made of knots, life's treasures are told.

Looming Shadows

In the corner a shadow begins to play,
A skip in its step, in a whimsical way.
It's stretched and it loops, like a soft, silly ghost,
Chasing shoes on the floor—it loves to boast.

Out pops a fringe with a shimmer and sway,
Whispering secrets from the light of the day.
It swings and it jives, doing a dance,
Begging the hat on the chair for a chance.

But oh the confusion when the broom comes to sweep,
And our friend in the corner starts shaking in sleep.
It hides in the fluff, giggling quietly,
For a broom is no match for its playful glee.

So when shadows appear with a skip and a hop,
Remember they're laughing at all of the flops.
In every odd dance, every twist and each sway,
There's a spirit of joy that won't fade away.

A Dance of Unraveled Dreams

Loose threads gather round for a spectacular show,
Each loop and each swirl is a marvelous flow.
They twine and they tumble in colors so bright,
Unraveling dreams in the soft, golden light.

One thread flirts with a needle, quite bold,
While another tells stories that never grow old.
They laugh at the snags, the pricks, and the tears,
In moments of chaos, they dance without fears.

A ribbon swings low, tipsy and giddy,
It spins with delight, oh isn't it witty?
Cameos of buttons join in the spree,
Making a bouquet of whimsical glee.

So join in the fun as the fibers unite,
In a dance of lost dreams that feel just so right.
For every stray thread wishes to be part,
Of a carnival of laughter, a tapestry of heart.

Threads of Belonging

In a closet where colors collide,
Stray threads dance, nowhere to hide.
A sock in the corner, with holes in its soul,
It laughs at the tales of the laundry's control.

Lurking in shadows, a ribbon retreats,
Dodging the scissor with nimble tiny feet.
Tangled with joy, in a box it does wait,
Hoping for partners—it won't hesitate.

A button once proud now spins like a top,
While crayons and patches create a big flop.
When sewing meets chaos in unplanned ballet,
A patchwork of laughter won't fray away.

With each cozy stitch, stories unfold,
Through seams that are silly and patterns so bold.
In this fabric of life, the quirks are the best,
For madness and memories weave a warm nest.

Corded Conflicts

Two cords entwined in a tangled mess,
Arguing loudly, oh what a stress!
One swears it will win and the other rolls eyes,
Mechanical bickering under the skies.

An old charger claims it's still worth a dime,
While a snazzy new cord thinks it's just prime.
They tussle and jostle with vigor and glee,
As dust bunnies cheer for their favorite spree.

The remote's lost in the bungle of blues,
Under couch cushions, laying out its clues.
They twist and they turn, a chaotic dance,
Intent on proving who's got the best chance.

In the end they concede, both tired and frayed,
Tangled in laughter, the conflict delayed.
With a chuckle they rest, in a cozy embrace,
For even the cords need their moments of grace.

Sown with Care

Threaded with giggles, the fabric takes shape,
A patchwork of whims, the artist's escape.
With needle in hand, a whimsical fight,
Colors clash boldly, creating pure light.

Stitches that wiggle, loops that sing loud,
Each snip and each seam makes me laugh out proud.
A snazzy creation from scraps left behind,
Sown with a heart where fun always shines.

In the scraps of the morning, the evening's delight,
Whispers of humor in every stitch tight.
Twisting and turning, the yarn plays a tune,
Bouncing off walls like an overjoyed loon.

From mishaps and mayhem, the fabric emerges,
A quilt of pure laughter and playful urges.
For every thread shares a chuckle and cheer,
In a world so sewn, with love and good cheer.

Threads of the Forgotten

In the back of the drawer, a ribbon lies low,
Dreaming of parties and big bows to show.
A whispering thread, once vibrant and bright,
Now ponders its role in the fabric of night.

The buttons have stories, they spin like a tale,
Of coats that once twinkled while they set sail.
A lonely old thimble is rusting away,
Still hoping for moments to join in the fray.

Crumbs of old yarn, where memories sleep,
Gathering dust in a corner so deep.
A patchwork of silence, but funny it seems,
They keep the past alive in their stitching of dreams.

So here's to those fibers, so shy, so discreet,
Who giggle in shadows yet dance to the beat.
For in every forgotten potential awaits,
A thread full of whimsy—the best kind of fate.

Laced in Laughter

A shoelace danced with a sock,
Tangled in knots, what a shock!
The cat jumped high, with a flick,
Chasing dreams, oh so quick!

Laughter erupted from a shoe,
Claiming it's got quite a view!
Each twist and turn was absurd,
As giggles were cheerfully heard.

A ribbon joined the mad parade,
In a twist, they all charade!
Silly antics on the floor,
Who knew knots could bring such score?

With colors bright and tales spun,
This playful dance has just begun!
So grab a thread, join the spree,
In a world of knots, we're all free!

Strings of Connection

Two yarns met at a cafe,
Sipping tea in a blurry way.
They laughed at puns tied in bows,
As fabric stories wove their prose.

A needle laughed with a thread,
"Let's stitch a tale!" it gleefully said.
Through ups and downs, they spun around,
Finding joy in the slips they found.

Bobbins spun with wild delight,
Creating chaos, not too tight!
With every loop, a giggle grew,
In the threads of life, joy broke through.

In a closet full of dreams,
A rainbow burst, bursting seams.
Strings of laughter braided too,
Connection in the patterns grew!

Friction of Fate

A scarf in a twist, what a sight!
Tangled in laughter, it took flight.
A tussle with gloves, what a tease,
Their quirky dance aimed to please!

Tangled shoelaces played a game,
Every trip turned into fame.
With a flip and a swirl, oh dear,
Who tripped who? We'll never clear!

A knot in the chaos, bright and proud,
Wearing confusion like a shroud.
The mishaps spun their own tale,
In a world where laughter won't fail.

Through fabric dreams and playful fate,
Every twist, oh, isn't it great?
With every loop and sigh of fun,
In this dance, we all are one!

Embroidered Echoes

A patchwork of giggles ran all around,
In a fabric shop, surprises abound.
Stitching a story with threads of cheer,
Every needle point brought us near.

A button bounced with a jolly grin,
Saying, "Let's see who can join in!"
With each whimsical tug and pull,
Laughter erupted, hearts were full.

Embroidered tales danced on the wall,
"Come play with us!" they'd joyfully call.
With every thread, a new joke spun,
Each little mishap—oh, what fun!

So gather your threads, don't be shy,
In this tapestry, together we fly.
With echoes of laughter entwined,
In the weave of life, our hearts aligned!

Colorful Confessions

In a world of hues, bright with glee,
One sock's missing, where can it be?
The dog wore it once, oh what a sight,
We laugh 'til we cry, deep into the night.

The curtains dance, they wiggle and sway,
They gossip at dusk, while children play.
Spaghetti stains, oh, what a riot,
Labelled as art, we won't start a diet.

A rainbow's mishap, a muddled bouquet,
Threads tangled together, in disarray.
Each color a tale, woven with fun,
Laughter's the needle, the day's work is done.

We're all just patches, stitched for a laugh,
In this quilt of nonsense, we find our path.
So grab a thread, let's weave it anew,
For who needs perfection, when we're this crew?

Fabric of Moments

A yard of joy, stitched left and right,
Quilted laughter sparks joy in the night.
One patch of chaos, another of cheer,
Each square a moment, oh so dear!

A pillow fight's fluff scattered in limelight,
Pajama-clad bandits, oh what a sight!
Giggles and dreams wrapped tight in a hug,
Like candy and cinnamon, snug as a bug.

Threads of absurdity crisscross our days,
With fabric so soft, it paves the ways.
To tales of triumphs and mischief galore,
The seams keep us grounded, while imaginations soar.

So let's gather our scraps, and craft a new tune,
In a world spun from laughter, we'll dance by the moon.
For in tangled endeavors, we find all the fun,
Together we'll stitch, till the day is all done.

Interlaced Spirits

Two threads entwined, a curious pair,
One's full of grace, the other's a scare.
Silly adventures in every loop,
These fibers of fate wrap up in a scoop.

A feather and rock, just can't get along,
Wiggling and jiggling, they sing a new song.
Patches of mirth, with tales to tell,
Each knot's a giggle, casting a spell.

From seams of the past to stitches ahead,
With each bit of fabric, new mem'ries are fed.
Spectacles funny, oh what a scene,
Dancing through life in this patchwork routine.

Under the fabric, we flourish, we grow,
With laughter the thread, we sew to and fro.
Let's twirl with the colors that life has gifted,
And cherish our chaos, in joy we're uplifted.

Bound by Threads

In this tangle of fibers, we stumble and trip,
Our shoes tied together, a comical slip.
Up and down streets, a laughter parade,
Entangled in joy, oh the memories made!

Two spools unwound, in a jester's embrace,
Dance like a fool, with no sense of space.
With every twist, the fun only grows,
Life's a wild craft, as everyone knows.

Stitched up in chaos, with giggles to spare,
A fabric of friendship, beyond compare.
Upon this wild mat, we tumble and weave,
In knots of hilarity, we live and believe.

So here we declare, with joy so profound,
Each fiber's a story, laughter unbound.
We're bound by our threads, in this merry ol' spree,
Creating a tapestry of pure jubilee!

Hues of Harmony

Colors clash in silly ways,
Patterns swirl in wild displays.
A purple dot on orange stripes,
The fabric dances, oh what types!

A quilt of giggles, laughter's thread,
A patchwork tale that must be read.
With every stitch, a joke is spun,
In this grand loom, we all have fun!

Looming Shadows

In the corner lurks a thread,
It wiggles, shakes, and scares instead.
A fabric ghost, with comical sights,
It makes us laugh through all the nights.

With every knot, it tells a joke,
A playful twist, a simple poke.
The shadows dance, the stitches cheer,
In this weird world, there's naught to fear!

Weaves of Time

In a twist of yarn, we find the past,
A weaving way that's sure to last.
The future's threads, they tangle tight,
Creating fabric, oh what a sight!

Each loop, each weave, a ticklish cue,
Laughing at clocks, as if they knew.
With every tick, our yarns entwine,
In this fabric dance, we laugh and shine!

Twirling Fabrics

Spinning round in vibrant glee,
The cloths come alive, can't you see?
With a whirl and a giggle, they leap about,
Creating a whirlpool of silly clout.

A twist of linen, a denim jig,
The fabrics play, oh what a gig!
Jesters of the thread, they spin and play,
In a dance of laughter, they bright our day!

Stitched Sagas

In the corner, threads entwine,
Colors clash, it's all divine.
A cat leaps high, and chaos calls,
And yarn cascades like shadowed falls.

Grandma's laughter fills the air,
"Who can tame this snarly hair?"
With every tug and twist and pull,
We create a quilt so wonderfully full.

A Mesh of Memories

Once I lost my crafty way,
My stitches danced, then went astray.
A stray dog found my tangled skein,
And chewed it up without a strain.

In every knot, a story lies,
Tales of triumph and some sighs.
Stitch by stitch, the laughter grows,
As every mishap brightly glows.

Twine of Hope

A whimsical twine with a bouncy hop,
Hitches and knits, then just won't stop.
Dancing fingers, the loop's too tight,
Saying, "What's stitched just feels so right!"

My buddy says, "You craft with flair!
With each odd twist, you conquer air!"
But tangled logs on a sunny patch,
Simply make the giggles hatch.

Patterns of the Past

Knots like stories, each one a twist,
None too easy, none to miss.
Walking back through stitches vast,
I wonder how we grew so fast.

With every tangled, lawnmower wreck,
Comes the joy on the craft board deck.
Silly projects, smiles galore,
In every jumbled yarn, we soar!

Interlaced Narratives

In a world of jumbled threads,
Knots and quirks, where humor spreads.
A sock says hi to its long-lost mate,
While laughing stitches twist and skate.

Loop-de-loops and bobbles too,
Knitting troubles, all brand new.
The yarn ball rolls, catches some dust,
As silly tales mix, we must trust.

Once a scarf, now a looped hat,
What on earth are you, old cat?
Each weave reveals its own strange tale,
In this fabric realm where giggles prevail.

So grab your needles, come and play,
Let's tangle up in fun today.
With twists and turns, we'll laugh and sigh,
As our loom of laughter spins up high.

Threads Beneath the Surface

A coat of many colors spins,
Hidden yarns with silly grins.
Underneath, a secret song,
Where mischief sings and dreams belong.

A button winks at an errant thread,
"Remember me?" it playfully said.
As tangles dance in joyous cheer,
The fabric whispers—'come near, my dear!'

Beneath the seams, a tale unfolds,
Of wobbly stitches and laughing molds.
A patchwork quilt of giggles bright,
Entwined with jokes, oh what a sight!

So lift the hem, peek inside,
Discover the fun we often hide.
For every thread holds laughter's charm,
In layers of joy, where we're all warm.

Threads of Whimsy

Spools of laughter roll away,
As puns and giggles come out to play.
A misfit yarn with a twisty tale,
Ticks the clock as we set sail.

Bobbles bouncing, skipping fast,
Crafting smiles that surely last.
Each stitch a wink, each knot a hug,
In this fabric world, we all just shrug.

What's this mess? A woven dream!
A hat of cats? Or so it seems.
Tangled threads create delight,
As we laugh until the dawn's first light.

So thread by thread, we weave our cheer,
With every tangle, we draw near.
In this whimsy, we find our place,
Laughing together in this warm embrace.

Frayed Edges of Memory

In a quilt with edges frayed,
Lies a story, not quite laid.
Each patch tells of laughter shared,
With gaping seams, still unprepared.

A sweater's story, a mitt's lost pair,
Woven whispers float in the air.
Though tangled threads may give a fright,
They hide the good times, pure delight.

Fraying fibers from years gone by,
A wink of color, a smirk nearby.
Memories tangle like strands of wind,
Each knot a chuckle, carefully pinned.

So raise a toast to the ragged seams,
To funny tales and wild dreams.
For in these frayed edges, laughter flows,
In the messy beauty, our joy grows.

www.ingramcontent.com/pod-product-compliance
Lightning Source LLC
Chambersburg PA
CBHW070305120526
44590CB00017B/2567

Original title:
Ties and Tales

Copyright © 2025 Creative Arts Management OÜ
All rights reserved.

Author: Lila Davenport
ISBN HARDBACK: 978-1-80586-016-7
ISBN PAPERBACK: 978-1-80586-488-2

Fables of the Interwoven

In a forest where stories bloom,
Lived a squirrel with endless room.
He gathered nuts, forgets with glee,
How many sit in his old tree?

The owl hooted, wise and bold,
"Your stash could fill a cupboard gold!"
But the squirrel just giggled and danced,
In his nutty world, he pranced.

Weaving Through the Ages

An ancient spider spins her web,
With flaws that make her friends just ebb.
The flies get caught, then break free,
"Check your threads," they buzz with glee.

A bee flew by, took a detour,
Got stuck in lace, then found a cure.
"You spin a tale as thick as glue!"
The spider laughed, "What's old is new!"

The Network of Our Lives

In the garden, gnomes sat tight,
Swapping tales from morn to night.
One claimed he once caught a star,
While another said, "You've gone too far!"

With every giggle, the daisies danced,
As gnomes exchanged their odds and chance.
"Last week I found a shoe, all red!"
"Did you wear it?" "Well, only a dread!"

Tapestry of Whispers

In a town where the whispers flew,
A cat sang to a sleepy shoe.
"Why do you snore? Shall we discuss?"
The shoe replied, "It's quite robust!"

A hog in a hat joined the debate,
"Do shoes have dreams, or just fate?"
They giggled hard, their tales entwined,
In a tapestry of thoughts defined.

Bonds of Forgotten Stories

In a cupboard, old socks reside,
Whispering secrets of days gone wide.
Missing buttons and mismatched pairs,
They still laugh at life's funny snares.

A cat sneaks in with a glittery ball,
While grandpa recalls his great wall fall.
The tales get taller, the laughter roars,
As we juggle myths and unclaimed chores.

Echoes of Entanglements

Two spoons fought over soup one night,
A spatula claimed it could take flight.
The forks were giggling, had no say,
As spatters of sauce led the way.

Old shoes hid behind the closet door,
Whispering tales of dances and more.
While mismatched laces skipped to the beat,
Together they made a rhythm sweet.

The Fabric of Memories

Patches of fabric with stories sewn,
A quilt that thinks it's a king on its throne.
Stitches unravel when the grandkids play,
Turning bedtime into a broadway display.

A thread once said, 'I can't take it straight,'
While buttons just laughed at their tangled fate.
Each fold a giggle, a playful scheme,
Crafting a patchwork of silly dreams.

Unraveled Narratives

Once a story began with a hat,
That talked and danced like a silly cat.
It claimed it was royalty, come what may,
But fell off during the grand parade.

A pair of mittens got caught in the spree,
Fighting over who would hold the key.
They jiggled with giggles, missed their chance,
In the end, they both joined the dance.

Silken Narratives

In a cupboard, yarns take flight,
A cat's chase brings tales to light.
Granny's sweater grows a cat,
Knots on the needles, imagine that!

Each stitch a story, laughter flows,
Who knew fabrics came with prose?
The fabric of life, oh what a tease!
Tangled and twisted, with such great ease!

The Story in Every Knot

A sailor's knot with secrets bound,
It whispered tales, both lost and found.
A sailor's tale of fish so grand,
But all he caught was seaweed band!

Tie your shoes, secure your fate,
But trip you might, on humor's plate.
Laces flying, what a sight!
Stories dance, by day and night.

Legacy in Loops

Round and round, the loops do spin,
Each turn a giggle, where to begin?
Grandpa's belt flung high and low,
A flag for practice, don't you know!

With every twist, we laugh anew,
A loop that links me and you.
Fables in fibers, snugly wound,
In laughter's grip, we all are found!

Tales Spun from Heartstrings

From heart to heart, the wool unwinds,
Stories woven, laughter finds.
A patchwork quilt of quirky dreams,
Each snip a giggle, or so it seems!

A rogue thread dancing out of line,
It claims the floor, "It's my time to shine!"
With every weave, together we grow,
In this fabric world, let the fun flow!

The Script of Shared Existence

In a world where socks go missing,
We laugh at every twist and spin.
Pants with holes and shirts with stains,
It's all part of our silly gains.

Friends who snort when they laugh,
Share snacks and even half a gaffe.
With hiccups echoing in the night,
We write our script in pure delight.

Patterns of Affinity

Like puzzle pieces gone astray,
We dance in a quirky ballet.
Choosing crazy hats to wear,
Creating chaos in fresh air.

Matching socks but different shoes,
In our club, there's no such blues.
Patterns clash in a vibrant spree,
Our mismatched lives fit joyfully.